Norman Jope

The Book of Bells and Candles

First published in 2009
by Waterloo Press (Hove)
95 Wick Hall
Furze Hill
Hove BN3 1NG

Printed in Palatino 11pt by
One Digital
54 Hollingdean Road
East Sussex BN2 4AA

© Norman Jope 2009
All rights remain with the author.

Typesetting © Matilda Persson 2009
Cover image © Lynda Stevens 2009

Norman Jope is hereby identified as author of this work in accordance with Section 77 of the Copyright, Designs and Patents Act 1988

This book is sold subject to the condition that it shall not, by way of trade or otherwise, be lent, resold, hired out or otherwise circulated without the author's prior consent in any form of binding or cover other than that in which it is published and without a similar condition including this condition being imposed on the subsequent purchaser.

A CIP record for this book is available
from the British Library

ISBN 978-1-906742-06-5

By the same author

In the Absence of a Summit (Phlebas, 1992)
For the Wedding-Guest (Stride, 1996)
Terra Fabulosa (Phlebas, 1999)

Contents

I. 'you, eye-fingered farness'

Distance	15
Hauptmarkt	16
The Five-Faced Tower	17
Waldweben	18
Bohemian Shore	19
The City of Alchemists	20
In the House Of Life	21
Small Change	22
Vibrato	23

II. 'Upon the spiral staircase/your dress rustles'

Clasp	27
High Tide	28
Residues	29
Mint	30
Apparition	31
Assignment	32
Cure	33
Stranger	34
Death-in-Life	35

III. 'Where do you come from?' 'I come from nowhere'

A Reflexive Interlude (1)	39
Hotel Hutnik	40
At the Corner of the Map	41
The Pole of Continentality	42
Zero (for an hour)	43
Widow's Peak	44
Bastions	45
Control	46
Fugitive Gods (1)	47

IV. 'Submerged in my fate I barely heard/the surface chatter...'

Paths	51
Toll Road	52
Panoramic	53
Fugitive Gods (2)	54
Oven	55
Neon	56
A Widow's Coin	57
The Happiest Barracks	58
The Ice Maiden Surfaces	59

V. '...melancholy, the dominant note'

A Reflexive Interlude (2)	63
Gran Mass	64
Wild Geese	65
Verfallen	66
Bocco di Veritas	67
Nocturne	68
Reunion	69
'Windless, Starless Night'	70
Cloisters	71

VI. 'The final word has not been spoken'

Fugitive Gods (3)	75
Maze	76
Heimat	77
Nunc et Semper	78
A Reflexive Interlude (3)	79
Flow	80
The Museum of Typography	81
Fountain	82
Luggage	83

Afterword

*For Gabriella: my fellow-traveller,
hostess and mistress in these parts*

The Book of Bells and Candles

I

'you, eye-fingered farness'

DISTANCE

The train jolts, waiting for a platform
at the edge of the City of Masters,
toys and poisonous tongues long-stilled.

Wind's brunt is elsewhere
and face-slapping rain.
The island's noise, at last, is out of range.

We've sailed steel rails to the core,
pecked at maps with a seagull's hunger —
eyeing the gabled farms and un-hedged fields,

drawn to the weight of land, to a Book
that's conceived in time-deepened space
from its spires and castles, its prophetic names.

Repeating the forehead word
I say goodbye, as I disappear
behind his string-driven movements —

distance inside us, map-spread
as the station sign unfurls, and I send him walking.
As soon as announced, the Book begins.

HAUPTMARKT

So, in shade, he sits,
at the heart of *das Reich*,
a postcard Tarot dealt from his hands.

As bratwurst, heretic-griddled,
enters his nasal sluices,
he inclines his beery head.

Almost all he sees is fake,
less real than in Riefenstahl's tarnished lens —
but this is still, no less, the place

from which, spread tracks to other cities
with distant, wolf-proof walls
and hardened shadows of hills.

Across miles and years
the bells resound in towers,
the candles melt in taverns.

I'll convey him east, in woodcuts.
Deeper then, that deck,
and the Book's expanse.

THE FIVE-FACED TOWER

He climbs to the five-faced tower
past spires and pan tiles,
steep-roofed houses on either side.

Crimson clouds turn violet.
Up here, the air
is dense with ghosts

of immolated women, still smeared with their soot
and under the surveillance of the five-faced tower,
the view contracts to the soles.

And later, on the bridge,
he looks down again and sees the stones,
a shoal from which the river retreats.

There are no more watchmen to cry the hours.
In the mild of evening, crowds assemble,
the dead ones mingling with the soon-to-be-dead.

But history's outside him, the purpose-born —
as loose and ephemeral
as love-songs busked.

WALDWEBEN

I guide him from the city, into the spruce.
How good, the forest coolness. If there are parasites,
he does not care. If wounds, he fails to notice.

A woodland bird flies up to him, her species uncertain.
She is female, he can tell from the veils in her voice.
She sings against the drum-roll of his feet in foliage.

A lizard flashes. He is stunned by its speed.
September sun makes sparkling patterns.
How good to stretch, absorb the birdsong.

Far from his mould, an imperfect substance
he re-invents origin, discovered in the wood
at the back of the mirror… what better place to start from,

to invent a life that knows both space and journey,
as a seeker, minstrel, freshman and fool?
How bright, her plumage. How mutable, the shadows.

He is lured by dreams of encountered twins
that appear like birds, with secret languages
precise and immaculate, seductive yet opaque.

BOHEMIAN SHORE

And, beyond the border and its sad bazaar,
trees retreat to time-glades
that the motorway can't reach —

plastic toys and brothels,
service areas and signals
fall from his eyes like film.

He enters, instead, a land that stretches
from the coast of Bohemia, with no sail in sight,
having surfed a wave of earth and straw.

Snow's underground, in its white abyss.
Harvested birds flail upwards.
I offer him these miles, horizons he accepts.

On the opposite seat, gold hair,
an apple scrunched, a scarlet jersey —
the visible realm, sweet ghosts.

The road into the city is a spiral staircase,
winding through suburbs, to the shore
of a river crossed in a glance.

THE CITY OF ALCHEMISTS

The city lies on its river of silver.
The steps lead to the visible Hrad
in which invisible twins reside.

She, who opposes time with love,
is still a whitened form, a negative of shade.
In a golden lane, alchemists grind

the body of their child and water flows
beside successive towns, the quarter of the Star.
Here, all energies are cast in stone.

He has entered it, unannounced,
with a silent joy in his own arrival
as the sun lights up the tiles —

as other mannequins cross time's face
to applause from tourists, and the square
condenses Europe to its carnival stalls.

Revived by tawny waters,
he enters more deeply, crossing a bridge
where statues erode like words.

IN THE HOUSE OF LIFE

Stains, the branches fall
across the camera's lens
as his paper skull-cap wavers in wind.

Here, the illegibility of death
is opposed by chiselled signs
of lion, carp or swan —

denoting earth bequeathed
to narrow, obdurate ground,
to be stone beneath stone, a guise of absence

written over, in this sanctum
where stone and flesh aspire to gold
and dead-stones huddle behind high walls.

He circles, on clay-clumsy legs —
and I spare the phoneme
in his mouth.

There are keys here to decipher stones
but the Book remains
to be secured, and bound.

SMALL CHANGE

Cottages shrink, then become huge.
One moment, they're full of souvenirs —
the next with retorts, and the clenched space of stars.

Tourists clog the lane, obscuring stones,
then their husks are lost, like coins
on the dungeon's mottled floor.

When scale is fluid, the world becomes lunar,
its mass dreamt out in nervous signals —
this narrow street, a bridge where the dead walk backwards.

He anoints his envisaged life
in a deeper shade of gold, as yet unaware
of the power of silver, as he gazes down

through the grill to scattered coinage,
seeing only gold, the visible reward
too deep for perspective, at the base of the world.

But the music of the imprisoned violinist
was, in fact, the wail of a man under torture —
so he reads, clinging to his coins.

VIBRATO

The blood that floods the platform below
is mauve, against absinthe walls
and the silvery lodes of the rails.

The name Krizikova sounds like a woman,
not a place he has not seen, as consonants ooze
from the lips of an invisible guide

and it is as if she were already there,
walking pastel streets
beneath the full moon's spillage of light.

How untrue, to say that I gave him my skin.
I gave him my word — half-truth, half-death.
So he attends, the un-conceived

and un-conceiving, with his millstone mouth,
a jug in need of a polish, a clay form unrefined,
that has gawped at gables, at the tricks of many trades.

Leaden fool, he'll pace
the platforms of Europe, heavily-shod —
in search of his soul, the priest's pale daughter.

II

*'Upon the spiral staircase
your dress rustles'*

CLASP

The woman at the reception desk
of the pension smiles when he wishes her
a *dobrou noc*, but that's all there is to say.

And the woman who flaunts her flesh
as he waits at the Central Station
only embarrasses, with mute persistence.

But chance is alchemic.
She enters the compartment —
seeing his *anglicky text*, she smiles.

By chance, he enters this city more deeply
that shrinks on its low mountain of silver,
six hundred years from limelight,

then still deeper, to the mauve of wine,
her unexpected company, her widened eyes…
to her silvery hands, her twin-ship.

Beyond arrival, he is brought to life
as naked as she is, as the full moon's face —
as if he could lead me over its edge.

HIGH TIDE

Another monster clings to that silver mountain.
Inside it, a man with a turquoise cloth
is polishing apostles.

Its carapace pierces the air
with spines, its saintly antennae.
Inside, it's as cold as on the far side of the moon.

He sees hares and scorpions in blotchy moons
on paintings, virtues poised,
including chastity, to vault the aisles,

but he is not here to seek forgiveness.
He is here to fill his eyes with unnatural glories,
to balance a magic that has made him human.

The full moon tugs from beneath the earth
where traces of silver still exist
in passages that parties explore

like an underworld, in the garb of ghosts,
their white forms drawn to the moon submerged
in a chasm of crystalline water.

RESIDUES

A few yards from the fairground,
the air is stained with tobacco.
The white walls of a convent hide that industry.

He turns for the Chapel of All Saints.
At the bottom of the steps, the bones appear,
exhumed from earth they craved for.

It's as if the moon had left them there
with the silver, on its journey.
Bleached, they are traces of its light.

With the others, he clicks his camera.
The atmosphere's festive, for the living
are unable to know their death through bone,

can only perceive what they are not
with total relief, and partial amusement.
'Nothing to do with them', the bones are stacked,

make chandeliers and vessels,
make death unknowable, unlike her body.
So god-like he leaves, in a nimbus of tobacco.

MINT

Full moon turns the city to silver.
Silver the streets, their bodies,
the ghosts, the hammered moon-coins.

It shines down the mines,
through layers of dust and midden.
Its silver seeps through strata.

From the city of gold to the city of silver,
sky becomes leprous. In the house of bones
each bone's immured, all mass becomes marrow.

But here, tonight, there is no mortality
where death's rays are white and life's transfixed.
The city persists in argent dust.

His Sol, her Luna, float as they embrace
on a bed as solid as a cloud, near the opened skylight,
inscribing a Book that may not be written

yet exists, no less, as they sit on the train
and watch for hares in desolate fields
as tomorrow's light re-robes them.

APPARITION

Monks turn to logs in the crypt.
Narrow logs, no longer the size
of a man, but just the length of a limb.

They rest on slabs, like patients
who have fasted here for centuries,
all life dried out, the flow squeezed elsewhere.

By contrast, she-and-he
have been softened almost out of time.
They sit in Freedom Square, sip drinks

under cocktail colours of stucco
and monks move through their veins
in a liquid form, recycled.

But she leaves him here,
so easily,
she might be smoke herself —

and her promise of a second rendezvous
on the homeward loop of his journey
is a stiff thing, like a staff he twirls in his hands.

ASSIGNMENT

There is a shrine in the middle of the wood
where water is pure and air, so quiet
that a nervous lizard could dissect it

if it scurried over stones.
How bronze the leaves are. The gaze of a deer
is wreathed in rustling silence.

As twilight closes in, I sense you,
leaving blue footprints on fallen leaves
as a silvery bird flies into treetops.

I wait for you, pressed into the niche…
as the vase of poppies that I leave at your lintel
is tipped into the street by a playful dog.

I wait, until the ice of morning
glazes my brow, and the Book can't help us…
then licked by wolves, his dreams dissolve

and he's solid again, in search of breakfast,
weaving past news-huts, where the images
of her, and her, and her expose our assignment.

CURE

Later, trains take logs along the darkened valley.
Spruce and birch line up on hillsides,
limestone bluffs are exposed like bones.

A lake lies to the left, with a half-drowned church.
Ahead, a tunnel leads to mountains.
They fade and return as stratus wavers.

The line ends by a lake, in the shadow of granite.
Its water is clear and its reflections, soft —
chalets, deserted. The season's almost over.

Twelve weeks before winter, and the pilgrimage
is reaching its zenith, not far from the tree-line.
Above, the chain-climbs tackle the Infinite.

He imagines her hand as he circles the lake
as if she, too, were with him here —
but she will not open a door in the mountains

and rain on pine drips green into mud
as logging tractors part the gathering murk
on fur-coloured paths, in a scrawl of smoke.

STRANGER

The hotel is made of crimson plush —
the restaurant is comfortable, yet dead to its locale
and his footfalls echoed in the centre of town.

So he walks, as if toward a gunfight,
down the oldest street, past burghers' houses,
as mountains sail the lakes of his eyes…

but where are the burghers? Only students,
speaking one of the exiled languages
with its own name for this place,

are in these streets, and doors are closed.
Burnt leaves and faint tobacco
focus the air with deep brown scents.

He dines and returns
past the ice-hockey stadium, the flats and hoardings —
in his room, he works on the code.

To be on the trail of a Book
that can contain this landscape, summon it back
to any space or time. To be a stranger, yet a searcher.

DEATH-IN-LIFE

The castle is blank and leprous.
Its lower gate is closed. The red roofs of the town
are defined against the roll of soil.

His ascent of the track becomes
a proclamation of exile.
It squeezes praise from his lungs.

The brothers have ceased their quarrel.
Away from implements of death,
the land glides out of itself.

Seen from a town whose pitted pavements
creak with the steps of the poor,
its grail-skull dazzles —

Roma children look up towards him,
harvesters on hillsides.
He waves back, invisibly.

The only power he emits is his gaze —
the only flag he can wave is the map
he struggles to unfurl in the wind.

III

'Where do you come from?'

'I come from nowhere'

A REFLEXIVE INTERLUDE (1)

At the centre of the world,
inscribed on marzipan,
texts of succulence are thickly applied.

How unseemly and camp, this *dérive*
in an age too replete for enchantment.
"I wanted this to be more than 'this"

says the prompter/puppet master,
the Joel Grey look-alike
marshalling tights and barstools.

Yet from the relay-station of noise
that vaults the ocean, a jet-stream of logos,
chest-beats, gunshots, hoisted erections

from Europe's muscle-bound kid brother,
he escapes, and I through him
to a worn green duvet

sequoias old, away from fries and high-fives
and gods worn on the sleeves of the saved
to attempt (as if) to hide from their force.

HOTEL HUTNIK

As soon as he checks in,
experience turns to memory.
He looks down corridors, as if at the past.

The view from the ninth floor —
identical blocks, in tombstone rows,
positioned across the valley.

There's a shower in the room, but no toilet.
Hearing his footsteps on the hallway carpet,
he dreams of disbanded delegations.

The city has one main street, but two competing names.
He feasts on soya in a vegetarian restaurant,
is beckoned outside by an angry drunk.

All this has already happened, despite the bell-toned voice
of the station announcer, even-syllabled.
He paces the park with a plastic cup

as drizzle masses, far from its ocean,
with all space and history behind him
like a spat-out mouthful of feathers and fat.

AT THE CORNER OF THE MAP

White secrets recline on snowfields
above the cabins, far from his room.
Wooden decades pile up in sheds.

In clean rooms ready for ghosts,
grandfathers shuffle and yawn.
Redundant boundaries are sloughed.

He would like to traverse this chain
and cross the abolished counties, one by one —
Bereg, Ung and Ugocsa,

nailed to the ground by pines
as green-grey evenings close in,
as dogs fall silent, and bottles are unscrewed —

he wants a wooden church in a wooded valley
to display her eidolon, her hooded eyes
as night reveals its harvest, far from cities,

close to saturnine peaks, their angular granites,
wants no message to reach him, as he sits
on the stranger's bed, and ignites her name.

THE POLE OF CONTINENTALITY

As if at Verecke
where armies
crossed,

he thinks
dark woods,
not-there

with
not-there her,
in the mist at the pass

that parts, revealing
the green tide west,
to the clearing

in foam
where bedrock rose.
Es gibt — two words,

their generous bounty,
pollen
smeared on the hands.

ZERO (FOR AN HOUR)

Snowed-on firs
on a snow-covered hillside
creak, on the spine of Europe.

Tongues move, licking
snow from silence.
Magyar. Slovensky. Hutsul.

But he will not stay — he is homebound,
escapologist who picks the lock
of winter, scraping frost from metal

as she walks off into whiteness
like a snow-princess or a sacrifice.
Unable to follow, he sits,

dreams, as mercury plunges
and stationmasters in full regalia
salute invisible ghost-trains.

Image in a Book, of an image in a book
of white firs by a roadside —
of a place where only footprints melt.

WIDOW'S PEAK

On a pale green ridge in a fold of a map,
two gravestones are grasped by cool brown soil
like limpets of time, held fast.

One is straight, the other bowed, yet both are embedded,
pointing at the bones of the dead,
nutrients that grass drinks deep from,

held fast, in the way that this hooded woman
walking through grass, is fixed in blackness
except for her face and hands, both barely visible —

is fixed, as black as the gravestones are grey
on this pale green ridge, beneath a washed-out sky,
by a lens that leads this moment

to the Book that equates them, a vision field
in which the gravestones live, and she is dead,
the one who leads where they will follow...

ploughing the horizon's stars,
their extinct light, their shattered mirrors,
deep into terrestrial green.

BASTIONS

Sharpened buildings. Jagged skylines.
Beech and spruce. Wolves, trailing flocks
through the undergrowth, with cinnabar eyes.

In storerooms, flitches of ham
that have greeny-gruesomed with age,
outlasting besieger and besieged.

To be billeted there, behind locked gates,
walls turned outwards to a domain
where pieties can't hold…

but he is left outside, in search of a script,
fearful of monks' designs, of herders' calls,
caught in the Evil Eye of an autumn moon

as mountains close before him
and realisation dawns, that grace
is only a campfire or a watch-tower,

that fear of the forest is the secret of Europe
and that all the walls of monasteries and castles
were built against the howling of wolves.

CONTROL

In a gap between hills,
the train halts.
He sits, with a carriage to himself.

These lines on the map
can't divide the Book.
Her identity drifts likewise.

Papers explain who he is
to great-coated guards
with badges on their caps —

citizen
of a favoured nation,
sowing its seeds of plenty.

Everywhere, her
and her and her —
the names alone are specific.

He sits
as if
on the lifeline of her hand.

FUGITIVE GODS (1)

This is a land in which the falling light
remains in the forest, as toadstool and ruby,
wolf-gall and monstrance, silver ring and rack.

And where trees are felled, or scoured to ash
by corrosive rains, the light they trapped
remains in air, with the dust-motes of its dead.

Between Maharal and *menschlein*, light-waves reach.
I envy him his traipse, from my castle of drench
as the Atlantic photocopies itself

across my cagoule. The Book I seek
is being compiled on these wood-paths —
the Golem co-creates a Golem,

mud learns to dance, in the guise of ink
and, beyond sanctity, the earth sprouts eyes
and words that require no children.

Thus, it fills the eyes and ears
that feed the Book, the impossible Book,
as it sits on the shelf of the highest branch.

IV

*'Submerged in my fate I barely heard
the surface chatter...'*

PATHS

There are lizards and bat-shaped leaves —
invisible birds, whose songs are strange,
auburn perspectives, tinctured with gold.

Colours and signs mark paths…
a circle here, a triangle there.
Trees become signposts. A way persists.

But to lose it, failing the map's commands,
means to cross the paths of lizards,
to jostle birds and crease the flowers.

And soon, the whole of this hillside will be white
and leaves, as crisp as parcel paper.
Already, the year seems past its bedtime

and paths are as vacant as the passages
that are not approved, just gaps in foliage
where forest surrounds, as dense as a chronicle.

Now, he can only see the forest inside him
which I knew before the hour of his birth —
but the forest he is lost in is the size of a continent.

TOLL ROAD

Sunflowers droop in fields
between slow towns, and challenge the sky
with microphones of charcoal.

Rain and Tears and other standards
play on the radio as bodies fidget
in leather seats, as the sun goes down.

Between village and metropolis
marker posts count down
as maize-heads waver.

Godscapes of light unfold
as if from a shepherd's hat —
a trick, played on time's disgrace

by the blackened wing of a hand.
And the city, too,
is mapped in starlight.

As above, its fire-streams
flicker from bank to bank, as if
even light came clear, in the end.

PANORAMIC

From here, the city's a mode of blossom,
complete, unknowable, exquisite —
and a somewhere else, when he descends.

Names are scratched on bark.
He reads that on the 3rd July
in 1953, came Antal Hájdu

to this tree, or an impostor,
knifed his name and clambered inside it.
Perhaps he's the old man who mutters

next to the display board's mushrooms —
but he's probably down below,
a microbe amongst the building-bloom,

one name, one face, in the city's infinity,
one body, in the bodyland of Europe,
another Golem, a product of his age.

How small each particular, each human star.
Both he and she, no longer luminaries
but light-points, lost in the eyes of others.

FUGITIVE GODS (2)

He follows an old man down the path.
White mud hardens under his feet
as shadows float in his eyes.

He suspects that he knows
the place from where the bus will leave
for the city's delirium of signs —

but thinks of a woodcut of a stooped old man
following the moon-queen to where he knows not,
observed by indolent smiles.

Shadows lengthen, point at the city
as a dead stoat, flopped on the path
like a torn-out tongue, reflects his muteness

as he searches for one who becomes more lost
each time he scans the map,
who is only real, in so far as she melts

to leave him beside the landscape's names.
They raise his waxing life to the power of death…
as the old man coughs, and is gone from sight.

OVEN

Brick by brick, the reconstruction
leads to a place that appears more real
because it's been effaced

by fifty years, instead of five hundred,
by the feet of the living, more than of the dead.
He shuns expensive restaurants

to seek an opening, walk off the Dreher
as if he could dwell here, unlike the others
with their money-belts and distorted maps.

Across the river, the illustrious buildings
bask in their pomp and suburbs waver
in the plain's late heat, as afternoon burns.

In the town of Ofen, he is scorched
as sugary shop-fronts bake.
The past he assumes is a trail of ashes

on which the other tourists step
as fiakers trundle, depositing shit
and the sun stomps pentatonically, a felt-hatted peasant.

NEON

Then, on the other side, it's night
and neon goldfish flounder in streets
as the rain's vice tightens, at the entrance to the Metro

where drivers argue, inspecting damage,
flattened by water as crowds ooze past
to restaurant, theatre and bar.

They fill the city, making it move
as rain moves, and the Book expands
in tangerine drench, in posters and graffiti

on shutters of shops in nailed-down zones
the Metro leads to, ending where the lost
spread out their cloths like charts in subways

until patrols arrive, and papers are checked.
Honeycomb of night, the city's
drilled by a neon he drinks,

drowned out by signals, immigrant names
as its language taunts, already yielded
to the pimps and procurers of her absence.

A WIDOW'S COIN

He hands it over, blind
to any sense of its value, content
to smile, to appreciate her thanks,

to see what's there once again —
the pylons, Tesco and Smatch,
the copies of lad-mags, named

in all the Empire's successor languages —
but in that metal mirror, there's a cold bed
older, even, than the face of that barman

whose eyes sank into earth,
the husband she lost,
the bowed-headed, weary one

who fathered her son, her daughter
then died a decade early, like so many here
to leave her with only coins to spend

which were spent, and not recouped.
By accident, or fate,
is he handing one back?

THE HAPPIEST BARRACKS

Cinnamon-dusted walls
loom over viscous cars —
how swiftly speed runs into the gutter.

Grime's hosed off
but bullet holes still itch
on their pockmarked skin.

Desire wants its statues to rise,
to re-name tomorrow, but clip-joints fill
as traffic slurs by bridges.

In underground clubs, in stairwells
there are still tears, lovingly patented —
the world turns under our soles.

In the Lukács, a red-haired woman
gesticulates and shuffles her eyes,
a *paprika* reborn in the human world.

He takes out his camera, like a magic lantern.
'Here' he says, and 'Here'
as if holding up time's ceiling.

THE ICE-MAIDEN SURFACES

Reflections, at the station —
of a word, or a sentence, that's bereft
in glare from so many lights.

The city reclaims the poem.
Its balconies creak beneath the weight
of stars with attitude, as night descends.

Beneath two kinds of constellation
he sits and dreams, his glass half-filled.
What can be done with time?

I am happy for him to sit here, in the forest
of this so-called sinful city, vivid as a ghost,
at home on the earth, to the sound of bells,

where there's a logo, bright as a toddler's toy
as if a loud land chased him, hurling candies
across a pond, to the ramparts —

but he exists by her nakedness, those patterns
emphatic to his touch, no New Found Land
but human earth, deepened to draw him down.

V

'...melancholy, the dominant note'

A REFLEXIVE INTERLUDE (2)

A dream strewn over maps,
his steps express my exile —
and how far I seem to have walked from myself.

Roads thread like sutures
on a skull-sized globe
as land, unrolled, steps out from its names.

But still, its soil won't shield me,
however strong my *kávé*
or how pentatonic my tones —

and no matter how deep my loves
or how long my physical journeys,
and no matter with what feline steps

my anima prowls with her blonde hair shining,
and no matter how black the boots she wears
or how red her lips, how moist her crevasse,

the blue-grey whorls of her eyes,
the bell-domes of her breasts and her two big toes
won't help me, any more than invented gods.

GRAN MASS

The air inside the Basilica
is plump and purple.
As he spirals behind the *trompe-d'oeil*

that adorns its dome, he becomes a rat
on a heavenly treadmill, grinding his own soul
until the aperture opens

and he sees across tiles
and the river, newly-bridged,
to the flats on the far bank,

sees hills with fencing wounds of limestone,
the river's serpentine bulk,
a projected border marked on its suds.

Looking west, he sees
an aircraft, on its way to the island —
to the north, tomorrow's train

that might return him for good,
but he's too near to the sky to think of that now
and too far from the ground to close the Book.

WILD GEESE

Old Lake, where martins parry the air
and rigging chimes, in 'a city of wild geese'
that have yet to arrive, with the ice.

In the old town on the hill, barbed wire
is rusted, luminous, a mother-lode revealed
and burghers' dwellings reveal their cracks

to smooth light, by verges
of weed-poked lanes. Old Lake, old light,
old life... old men in the by-passed square

just sitting, in front of the Lottery shop,
their fortunes confirmed. Downhill
by lake-castle ruins, an Excalibur perspective

from a shabby bench is soundtracked —
Webern's Six Pieces, their Kakanian lament,
slide stolidly through his mind.

In the Café Barta, coffin-coloured wood
contains him for a marzipan feast,
beyond the lake that the migrants have not found.

VERFALLEN

Leaf-crunch, corpse-rattle,
paper-crackle, underfoot
like pages, warmed in hands

by frenzies of decoding —
then Princep's pistol, whiskers
brushing dust, consumptive

coughs in trenches, mud-gas-haze
where the sister waits,
greeting heads that roll

from Grodek and Isonzo,
laments spooled out of their mouths
in Gothic script, as they move

down rail-tracks mottled with rust,
down years of aftershocks,
false dawns and sunsets,

to lie like toadstools or chestnuts
here, at a schoolgirl's feet,
in dumbstruck gardens of autumn.

BOCCO DI VERITAS

From the Fire Tower's balcony, the roofs
are scarlet against green hills.
The town's a crab, asleep in its shell.

The music of Liszt, for whom
all Europe was both home and place of exile,
circles the walls like a hawk,

as dutiful tourists tick off sights
and trade-routes heal the border's wound,
its barbed-wire souvenirs already in cupboards

as cappuccinos thicken, and the Euro strolls,
a Disney character, from terrace to bank.
Yet, in back streets over the river,

stucco crumbles and the Moor's Head
opens its mouth on silence, yawning
like a psychopomp who's seen so many hells

that this genial place, this sequel to itself,
means only a cavity that's filled by dentists,
where bones are unsightly, and the past is *stumm*.

NOCTURNE

The white road leads to a village.
Night falls, to the sound of geese
in the violet pond. How frosty, their cries.

In the village, bells are silent
as a violin strikes up in the darkness of a tavern.
Blood moves slowly, in the shade of a church.

How heavy, the gravestones and their shadows.
A mouse flits, golden in the gathering twilight.
Names become illegible, their ghosts anonymous.

How good it is to wander into silence
when bells have ceased, the day redeemed
by blue sleep that follows, the amnesiac moon.

And, after so many moons, the village
settles down to another, slides from the map
to be vacant, nameless, hewn from air.

Tracing his finger in the dust,
he recovers the Book of Bells and Candles
from darkness, as if bound in his own true skin.

REUNION

In middle distance, the Altstadt
parades like the star of a Rococo painting.
Intriguing ghosts link arms in the garden.

In the palace, The Kiss reveals its blemishes
when seen from close up, but step back and it's perfect.
The Schieles flaunt their wounds, transcending their own revolts.

Silence cools around them, like cream-clogged coffee.
The light here is gold, the shadows mauve.
They feel the weight of the tracks they follow,

bound to each other by the dreams of this place —
lovers mass behind them, queue for oblivion,
with names the Book won't press into its pages.

Poppy and grain still bend
in built-on fields that were forest.
A silvery hand snuffs out a candle...

and he blushes, as if they were siblings,
severed by biography, yet joined at the hip
as if to reflect their reflections.

'WINDLESS, STARLESS NIGHT'

Her lean face, heraldic, leopard-starving.
His curiosity. His lust. His terror.
The shadow of his rival, no more than a breath

that creeps through a crack in the window.
She stretches as he scans the imagined city
through layers of glass, unable to relax

despite her feigned innocence, her offended charm.
Yet exhaustion, spiced with lust, returns him to her
and she rides him, lightning-haired, her pale brow shining.

No, he knows, this has nothing to do with death
and the shadowy man she calls her brother
is only the one who arrived before him,

to be shaped by her shadow, from another time
when the Book was as fresh as a young woman's skin
and the landscape vaster, so hard to cross

that it brought the infinite to every rampart,
stranded cities in a night
of wolves, and alchemists, and ice-studded stars.

CLOISTERS

To die. To prepare to die. To prepare to prepare to die.
To prepare to prepare to prepare… etc.
Lost in thought, he circles the cloisters.

Product of a world in which the sense of guilt
has outlasted sin, he cradles that stone.
How it loads his belly, like a wheel he is bound to.

He is guilty because he is not guilty.
He has ripped her out of his heart
because she deserves a home of her own.

How cool the light here, tinting cloisters
as his visit concludes, his feint at penance.
He leaves, with his shadow close behind him,

the printed shade of the rustling Book
he carries to the coach, her absence
bound and sealed and delivered —

but what of that? He must leave her behind.
The quarrel was cosmetic, the parting staged.
Her mercenary reasons were beyond reproach.

VI

'The final word has not been spoken'

FUGITIVE GODS (3)

Sky housed his height, that earth made tall.
Mortal, he moved through gelatines of time,
past men, past creatures, to their shine-steads.

She, the invented, waits imperious
on subway trains, in surgical malls,
surrounded by perfumes, by the gloss of flowers.

He, the clay-created, travels through
the same terrain, in love with its graffiti,
its swirling languages, its matt cafés

where, behind espressos, wait eyes in armies,
assignations, secrets, depths of amethyst —
all I want from him, to know that I am alive

but for only so long, and that life rarely is,
comes out of us as quickly
as the scripted statement of a hostage.

Sometimes, we meet the gods
or they leave their scales on our fingers.
Sometimes, we learn their names.

MAZE

She weeps from time to time, but that's
no more than melodrama.
In her heart, she remains playful.

She can wear a halo or hold a tower —
she can also cross her legs on the Metro
and impale a man on the thorn of her eye.

Here, she's the wise old man's albino daughter
but it's my decision, not her father's
to tear the *shem* from his mouth,

to fill his skin, once more, with clay.
He's walked his circle, almost — from square to square,
this stroller of myself, on a guided tour

from birth to truth to death
and, like any tourist, when asked to fetch apples
he returns with vendor, basket and stall.

When sent for a Book, what spaces he invades,
even as his errand fails, as it must —
what mazes, only he could stumble into.

HEIMAT

Labyrinth of painted dust,
of broken swords
and rusted ploughshares.

Chamber of the buried master —
of extinguished torches,
dusty thuribles.

Theatre of lunar roads —
of wolf-howl, boar-stench,
gathering thunder.

Space of palaces, aisles and altars,
markets, dungeons, steep-roofed houses,
streets of narrow stones.

Land owned, land conquered,
ceded and ravaged,
patched up and laid to rest —

its signs and banners traced
on air, like moonlight
soaked into morning.

NUNC ET SEMPER

A masked procession enters the square
with torches. I compel him to watch
as buildings loom, absorbing light.

In space death leaves, an unaccompanied song
drifts over rooftops, as drinkers perch
and savour the beer's burnt taste.

Ghost-blood flows in invisible runnels,
pursued by plague-rats. Broken on the wheel,
heretic futures are abandoned —

pulverised faces, slaves of delusions
sweeter than others, no fools but still nothing
he can cling to in this tableaux time

when buried bones are props
in our imagination, but the gables hang
for him alone, in the absence of hangmen.

Beside the burning ground, where ashes take flight,
he savours the smoky taste of her absence,
the Real he toasts, with a glass I hold.

A REFLEXIVE INTERLUDE (3)

Gods with nothing inside.
The Baptist to Salome —
'Du bist verflugt.'

In the middle of a dream, it becomes too clear
that the dream's a dream and, shaking with the chill
of mortality, one wakes.

In the mall, a voice
that wishes us Happy Shopping
comes at us, from beyond the fountain.

But consume your own fantasies
and you will be endless.
I don't care if they're damned.

The wanton teenage temptress
hides her eyes
in chasms of make-up.

Inside hollow gods that dazzled the Poet,
scraps for vultures and ravens.
Then the stork's flight, mapped in reverse.

FLOW

On a sunny afternoon, he summons the Book.
It lies by the river, in the shade of the Dom,
by the rain-brown river that moistens pages.

It is almost too heavy to lift
with the spirits it invokes, its titled dead
who cling to life, like lampreys to a boat,

from Old Europe's *wahn*
of gilt and sackcloth —
but she, who did not die,

who sleeps, in pursuit of freshness,
with blood still viscous on her lips,
graces ink and hones his strength

beside a river that will flow to its delta,
gathering reflections she could never cast,
from the swords of princes to the rings of bishops.

Yet he walks alone, as if this were ordained,
part thief, part wet-nurse of a Book
that pads through his head and pants like a wolf.

THE MUSEUM OF TYPOGRAPHY

The darkness of ink, the stamp of woodcuts.
The Book is finished, the museum locked.
The Book is concealed in the Open.

Apocalyptic horsemen hide in a street
that is thick with dust and vaporous lead,
but the Stone of the Philosophers is all around them.

Contained in the landscape, smelling of oak,
the City of Alchemists is crimson and gold.
The museum is a tomb, but the Book has escaped.

It is stone and wood, it is in the contours
on the wanderer's map, where wild boar forage.
It is under that shrine, at the top of green mountains,

and lost in a chamber where a walled-in woman
awaits her death, yet floats in the hands
of a ghost that sits on a crumbling step.

She appears opaquely, carrying the Book,
like a gentle student, across the river…
to touch her is to touch migrating birds.

FOUNTAIN

That twist of figures in the Hauptmarkt.
Water, splashing over them
that will freeze in a matter of weeks.

Blue beak spires ascend
behind stalls with gingerbread loads
and frames of resurrected windows.

As if nothing had happened, he addresses a postcard.
Nothing **has** happened. He has travelled
like a fly across a painting.

And that other land, the interior
gives way to thoughts of islands,
of sea that caresses as it buffets.

She crosses the square in a long black coat,
close to a dark-haired, dark-eyed man
who places his hand across the lens of the camera.

The words I have given him to store in his eyes
are like pigeons at war on cobbles
for scraps of *lebkuchen*, and some ground to rest on.

LUGGAGE

But the Book disappears in the night
although he had locked the room from inside
and slammed the shutters hard on the stars.

So he packs his bags and takes a seat
on a platform of the seedy station
where plain-clothes cops with earnest expressions

disguised as backpackers, turn on their suspects,
then send them off without apology
through grainy halls where the excluded loiter.

Best out of that. So I de-create him
and the landscape rolls, unbound,
a green sea splashed with vermilion sails

as I think back to the sidings
at the edge of the city,
twenty tracks, my train in the middle,

row upon row of rusting rails,
all the buckled trajectories
of other journeys.

AFTERWORD

Most of the pieces in *The Book of Bells and Candles*, which was composed between 2002 and 2005 and revised in 2006, refer to places visited; a few others, to places experienced indirectly, either through travelogues or works of literature. Although each of these pieces exists, hopefully, in its own locale, I, as a reader, would want to know where the 'evidence' had come from.

The visited places, therefore, are as follows:

Nürnberg: 'Distance', 'Hauptmarkt', 'The Five-Faced Tower'.

Praha: 'Bohemian Shore', 'The City of Alchemists', 'In the House Of Life' (*Josefov*), 'Small Change' (*Zlatá ulička*), 'Vibrato'.

Kutná Hora: 'Clasp', 'High Tide', 'Residues' (*Sedlec*), 'Mint'.

Brno: 'Apparition'.

Štrbské Pleso: 'Cure'.

Poprad/Spišská Sobota: 'Stranger'.

Spišský hrad: 'Death-in-Life'.

Košice: 'Hotel Hutnik'.

Budapest: 'Panoramic' and 'Fugitive Gods (2)' (*Buda Hills*), 'Oven' (*Buda*), 'Neon' and 'The Happiest Barracks' (*Pest*), 'The Ice-Maiden Surfaces' (*Nyugati tér*).

Esztergom: 'Gran Mass'.

Tata: 'Wild Geese'.

Sopron: 'Bocco di Veritas'.

Wien: 'Reunion', 'Windless, Starless Night'.

Bamberg: 'Nunc et Semper'.

Regensburg: 'Flow'.

Nürnberg (again): 'Fountain', 'Luggage'.

The 'Bohemian Shore' comes, of course, from Shakespeare's mistake in *The Winter's Tale*. The Hotel Hutnik is a real place, or was in 1998;

my ambition to visit every Sixties and Seventies high-rise hotel in the region remains, as yet, unrealised. 'Ofen' is the old German name for Buda and 'Gran' for Esztergom (as in Liszt's 'Gran Mass'). Tata's Old Lake (Öreg-Tó) is one of Central Europe's most important wintering sites for migrating birds — and Tata, therefore, promotes itself as a 'city of wild geese'.

The pieces from 'At the Corner of the Map' through to 'Bastions' concern Carpathian lands not yet visited at the time of composition. Two photo-albums have supplied relevant images; namely *Kárpátalja* (Tölgyfa Könyvek, Budapest, 2003), which covers the Trans-Carpathian Ukraine and *Erdély* (PéterPál Kiadó, Veszprém, 2002) which does likewise for Transylvania.

The sectional headings are from the following sources;

I — Paul Celan, trans. Michael Hamburger: from the translated poem 'The Irishwoman, mottled with parting...' (*Selected Poems*; Penguin Books, London, 1990).

II — Georg Trakl, translator Robert Grenier, from the translated poem 'Summer' (*Selected Poems*; Cape, London, 1968). The title of the poem 'Windless, Starless Night', and lines 13 and 15 of the preceding poem, 'Reunion', are also based on this translation (and on my halting knowledge of the original).

III — attributed to Andy Warhol (whose family came from Medzilaborce, in Eastern Slovakia), although the quotation also appears in *The Pursuit of the Millennium* by Norman Cohn (Paladin, London, 1970), attributed to an 'incorporeal image' that appeared to a C14 German mystic, Suso. Ultimately, of course, it is to 'no-one' that the quotation belongs.

IV — Attila József, trans. John Bátki, from the translated poem 'By the Danube' (*By the Danube*; Corvina, Budapest, 2002).

V — Claudio Magris, trans. Patrick Creagh, from the 'Café Central' chapter of *Danube* (Harvill, London, 1999). Magris' book has affected these poems, to a degree that goes far beyond explicit reference.

VI — Tilo Wolff, from the song 'Ein Hauch von Menschlichkeit' ('A Touch of Humanity') on the Lacrimosa CD *Echos* (Nuclear Blast, 2003).

Angelo Maria Ripellino's *Magic Prague* (trans. David Newton Marinelli; Picador, London, 1995) is another key source. My use of the Golem myth has depended on Ripellino's scholarship, although the way in which I use it is something I claim for myself (i.e. the tourist as a Golem; the self constructed in memory, or in the literary act, as a Golem; and so on).

Musical sources have also inspired me, from the work of the German electronic musicians Peter Frohmader and Klaus Schulze, and earlier classical composers such as Béla Bartók and Anton Webern, through to the darkwave of Lacrimosa and, perhaps most notably, an overlooked album by the Anglo-German darkwave group Love Is Colder Than Death, *Mental Traveller* (Hyperium, 1992). The journey I take, on hearing the first few tracks of this work, is — despite its origins — a Carpathian one. The line 'Du bist verflugt' or 'You are accursed (damned)' in 'A Reflexive Interlude (3)' comes, of course, from Richard Strauss' opera *Salome*.

As I am in the process of editing a Critical Companion to the writings of Richard Berengarten (formerly Burns), I should also confirm that the formal similarity of this sequence — consisting as it does of unrhymed, eighteen-line poems in six three-line stanzas — to that of his sequence, 'Following', which appears in his *Book With No Back Cover* (David Paul, London, 2003), is coincidental. Although I may have heard a few of the poems read in 2003, *Book With No Back Cover* first came to my attention in printed form in early 2005, three years after I started this sequence and began to circulate parts of it in earlier drafts — simply, I used this form to provide me with a flexible, slightly-more spacious alternative to the sonnet, whereas Burns uses it to relate to specific hexagrams of the I Ching. The stanzas of Aidan Andrew Dun's *Vale Royal* (Goldmark, Uppingham, 1995) may, however, have influenced the form of these poems, if unconsciously after a period of time.

Finally, the wilful untimeliness of this sequence can't be overlooked. In the course of its composition, I've often felt as if I were writing it, somehow, from an earlier time or, rather, from a time which has never been a 'now' but was never looking to be a 'now' in the first place. However, I'm glad to have followed my instincts, not least because I've never believed that the value of any creative act resides, intrinsically, in its responsiveness to the immediate demands and trends of the time in which it takes place, and also because I'm pleased, as a lifelong inhabitant of Europe, to have been born into the historical and geographical space it offers. This sequence, amongst other things, is a gesture of respect towards that space, from its Atlantic edge, at a time when — as a result of globalisation and demographics — it is in the process of changing, for better as well as for worse, beyond all recognition.

Norman Jope